T0365857

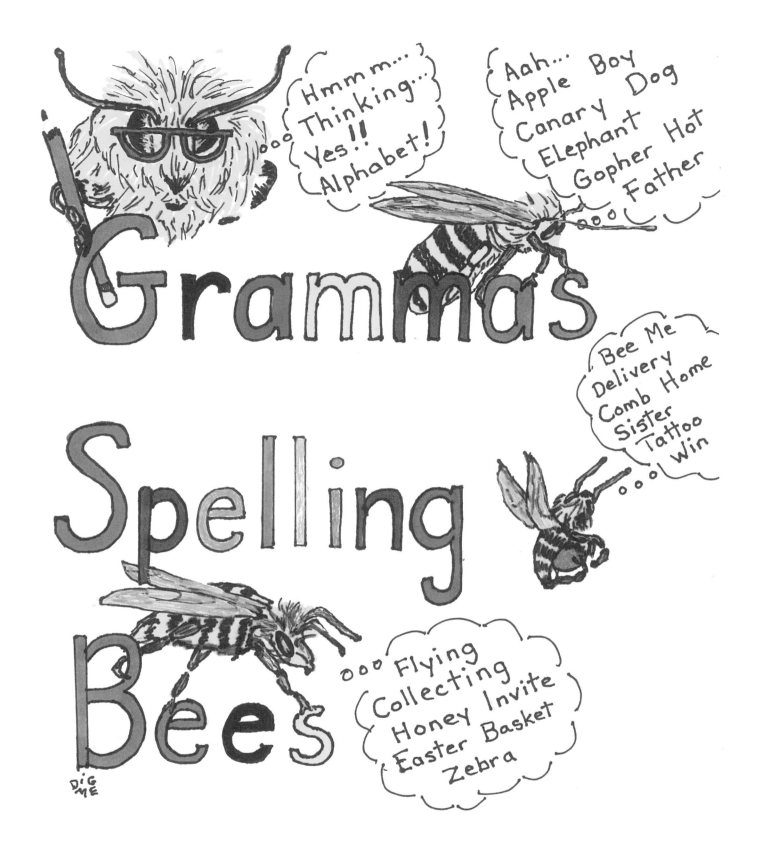

Gramma's Spelling Bees

A book for all ages.

WestBow Press books may be ordered through booksellers or by contacting:

WestBow Press
A Division of Thomas Nelson & Zondervan
1663 Liberty Drive
Bloomington, IN 47403
www.westbowpress.com
844-714-3454

Because of the dynamic nature of the Internet, any web addresses or links contained in
this book may have changed since publication and may no longer be valid. The views
expressed in this work are solely those of the author and do not necessarily reflect the views
of the publisher, and the publisher hereby disclaims any responsibility for them.

Any people depicted in stock imagery provided by Getty Images are models,
and such images are being used for illustrative purposes only.
Certain stock imagery © Getty Images.

Interior Image Credit: Mary Woodman

ISBN: 978-1-6642-0868-1 (sc)
ISBN: 978-1-6642-0869-8 (e)

Library of Congress Control Number: 2020920046

Print information available on the last page.

WestBow Press rev. date: 03/05/2021

WESTBOW
PRESS®
A DIVISION OF THOMAS NELSON
& ZONDERVAN

This book is, first and foremost, dedicated to God. He has always encouraged me to try just a little bit harder to do more for others… and to enjoy the life He has given me. He gave me my children, my grandchildren, and of course my great grandchildren…to inspire me to do something special for all of them. Not just MY family, but, all children. TO make it fun and interesting to learn how to spell small words, and big words, some of all words they will use at some point in their lives.

Enjoy my book children…parents…and all who assist in the joy of learning.

God love and bless you all.

Writing and artwork
By: Mary Woodman
A.K.A "Gramma Midge"

Reference book:
Webster's Dictionary

Instructions for playing the spelling game...

1. Choose a word from the index pages.

2. Spell the chosen word for the searcher(s). Have the searcher(s) spell it back to you.

3. Have the searcher(s) find the word on the correct page.

4. After 10 correctly found and spelled words, the searcher(s) receive a prize.

Most important part of this game is to learn spelling AND have fun at the same time.

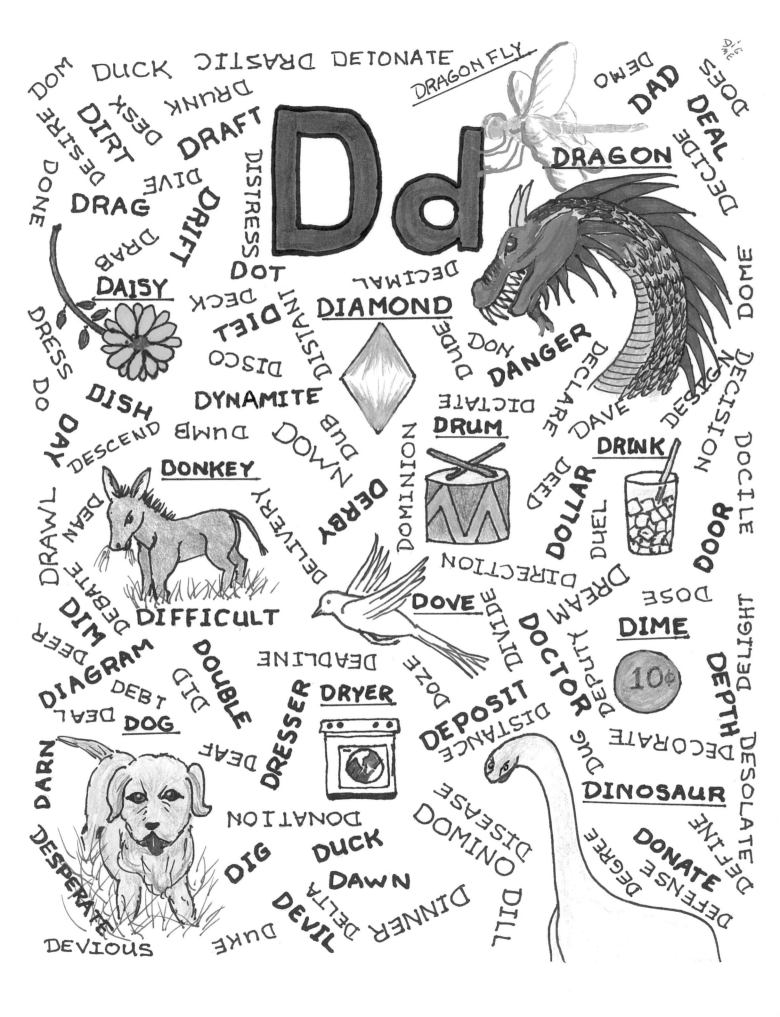

Gg

GHOST

GEOGRAPHY

GENERALLY GEL GENUINE GAME

GRIMACE GREY GROUND

GARLAND GENE GANG GUILTY GAP GAS

GREW GRADUATE GREAT GIRAFFE

GRADUATE GLOVE GO

GYPSY GENERAL GRUB GORILLA

GECKO GALOSHES

GALLERY GRAY GIBBON GIGANTIC GENIUS

GREY-GOOSE GRAPES GUIDE GIGGLE

GLORY GIFT

GUPPY GRAVE GRACE GALLOP GROWTH

GALE GENTLE GNOME GRILL GOOP

GIVEN GALLOP GOD GUARD GET GUMDROP

GADGET GERANIUM GIVE

GOLF GUN GRIME GATE GARDEN GEYSER GOPHER

GARMENT GOOD GLANCE GUM

GOT GREEN GUSH

GIRL GLASS GOSPEL GARAGE GORGE GOBBLER GARGLE GLAD

GAR GLOBE GOVERNMENT

GLEAM GOBBLE GYMNASIUM GAG GRASS

Ii

ICECREAM
INVENT
INVOLVED
INVITE
INNOCENT
INTO
INSCRIBE
INTRUDE
INSOLENT
INSTEAD
IBIS
IVY
INVOKE
IMP
IMPENDING
INSTANT
INVESTIGATION
INFUSE
INSPECT
IT
IDIOT
ICICLE
INHABIT
INTEND
IRIS
IMAGINE
INSPIRE
INK
INSECT
IS
IMMIGRANT
IRISH
IMPRESS
IGLOO
INSTRUCT
INFORM
ILK
IMAGE
IMP
IGNITE
ILL
INDEED
ITCH
ISLAND
IMMEDIATE
INDEX
IF
IN
INCLUDE
IMPOLITE
INSTALLED
IRONIC
IGNORE
IMPALA
ITEM
INTERFERE
INDIAN
IRON-MAN
INTERRUPT
INTERNET
INVOICE
INVALID
INTEGRITY
IMPEL
IMPAIR
IMMUNE
INCH
ISSUE
IGUANA
IMPOSING
IDEA
ISOLATED
IVORY
IMPOSSIBLE
ID
IMPRINT
INTEREST

L l

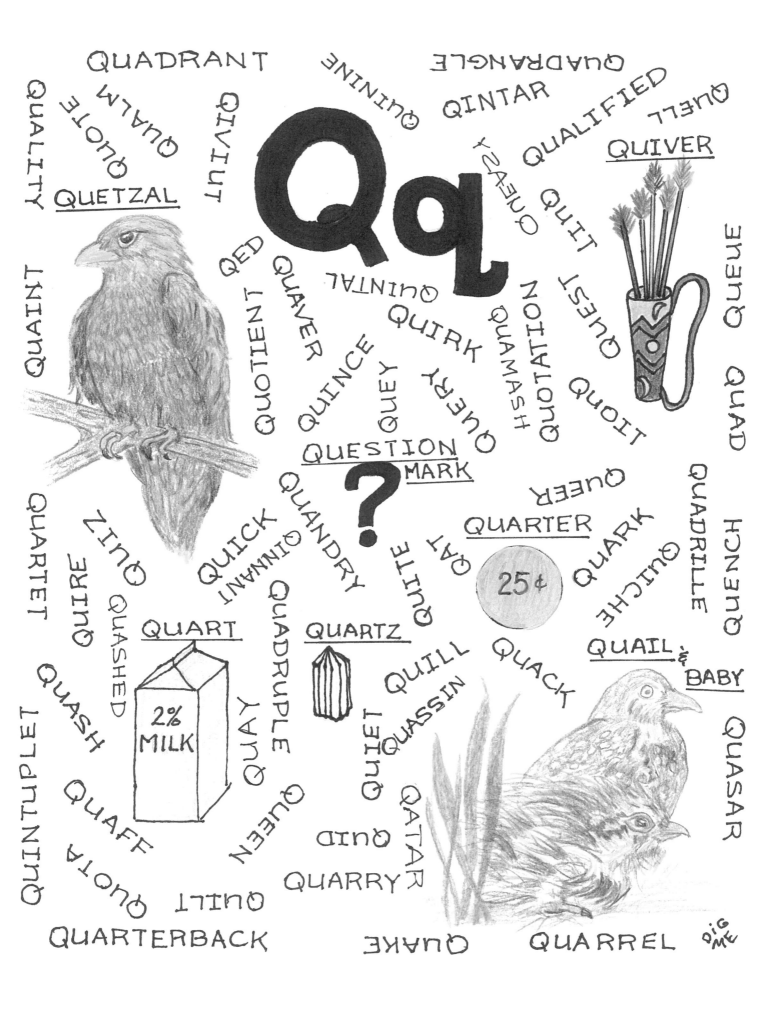

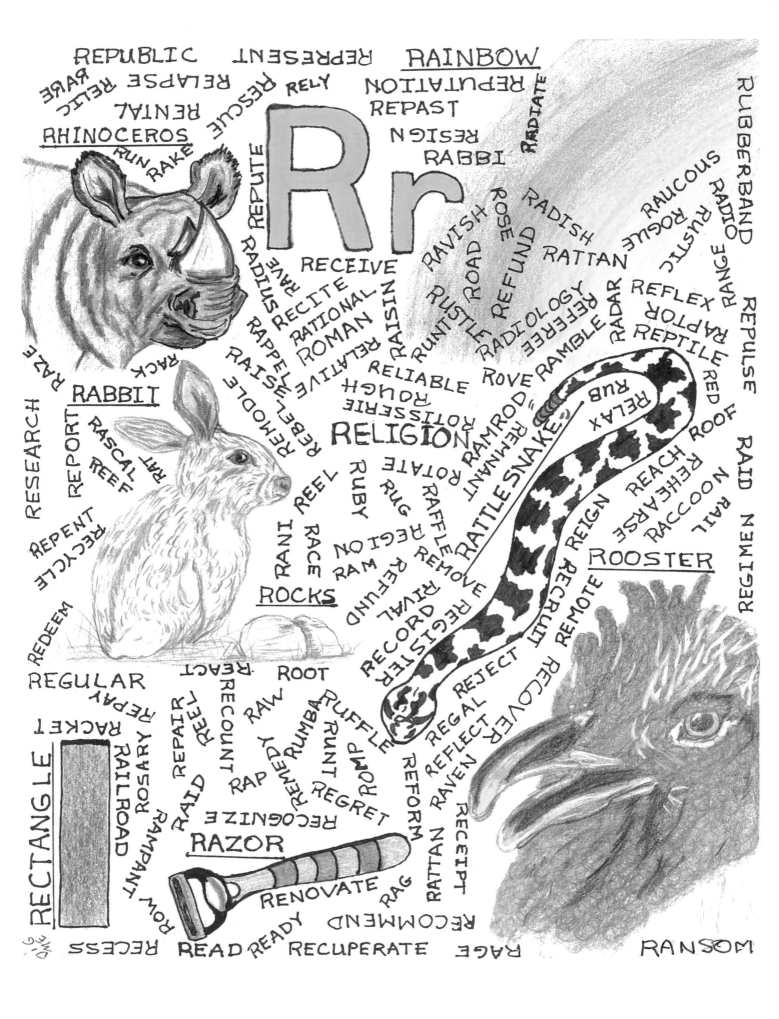

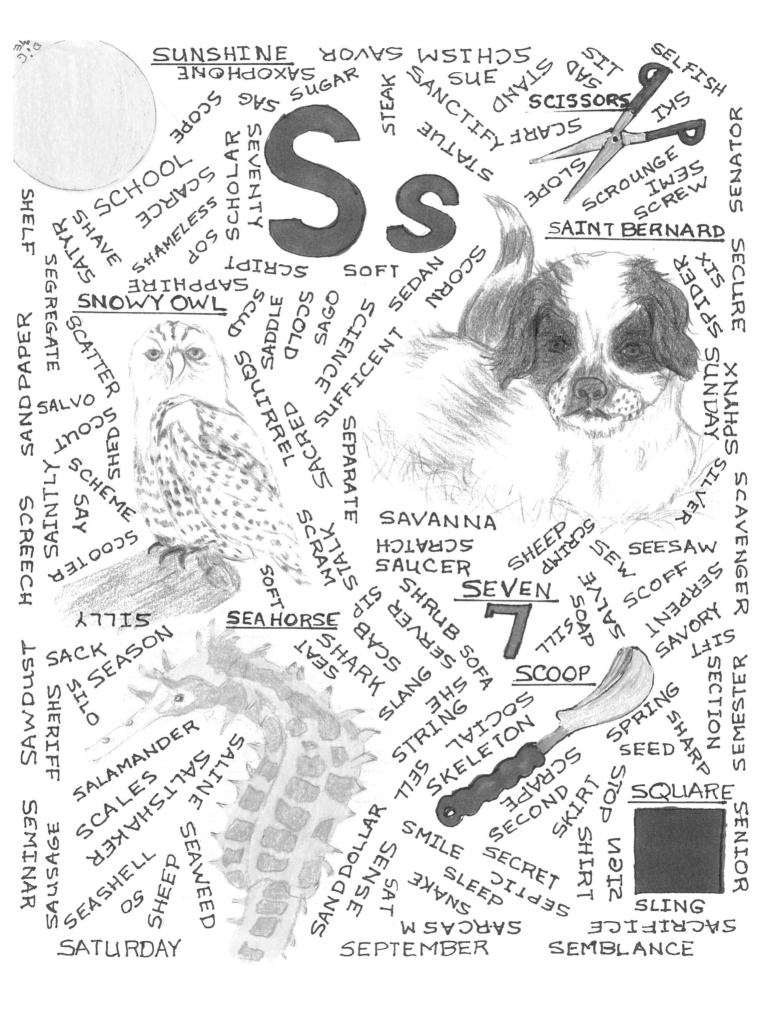

TWINE TELEVISION

TECHNICAL TEACH

TELEGRAM TWEED THRONE

TELEPHONE TREE TATTOO

TO TEAPOT TONSILS

TERMINAL

TASMANIAN DEVIL

TRANSFORM THOUSAND

TESTIFY TAVERN TEMPERATURE

TARNISH TERRAIN TAPIOCA

TUG TABOO TRIANGLE TIMBER TROUBLE

TURMOIL TARPON TAX TERRACE

TWIN THOUGHT TERRITORY

TANG

TT

TOILET TRIUMPH

TRITON

TRIVIAL

TORTOISE TRACTOR TEMPO

TOGETHER TWEEZER

TIGER TOTE

TRELLIS TEMPLE

TRAFFIC TENT

TAM

TREASURE TACKLE TRAVEL

TWILIGHT TODDLER TIP TODAY TILT

TULIPS

TEDDYBEAR TUMBLE

TRESPASS TWO

TOE TABLE TENNIS TUTOR

TONGUE TUNDRA TUBE TOO

TROUT TORCH TURRET

TRUCK TUNE TEMPER

TOUCAN TOWARD TRENCH THUNDER

TWINKLE TWICE TEN TWENTY

TOLERATE TWIST TROOP TELL TRIBUTE

TRICYCLE TREMBLE TOKEN

THANKSGIVING

TENDER TURKEY

TWIRL TELESCOPE TRUTH TITLE TILE

THUMB TARDY THEATER

TYPE TOMATO THROWN

TOBOGAN THEM

TENDON TRILOGY TOXIC FORTUNE TOOTHBRUSH TORNADO THINK TRIFFLE TOUCHE TURBAN TRY

TOGA TIARA

TWELVE TOMORROW

TIRE THERAPY

TOURNAMENT TICKET

TETRA

TITANIC TATTOO TAILOR TOAST TUNIC TOAD TRASH THESE

TOM·TOMS

TREND THEY

TOPIARY

TALISMAN TIZZY PIG

TUESDAY

TREASURE

TREAT TRICK

THURSDAY

Uu

URSA
UNCOMMON
UNDERGROUND
UNDERFOOT
UP
UNIQUE
URANIUM
UMBRELLABIRD
ULTRA
UNANIMOUS
UNCANNY
UTILIZED
UGLY
UNICYCLE
UPRISING
UNZIP
UNDERSTAND
USE
UNHAPPY
UNTANGLE
UNPREDICTABLE
UROLOGY
UTILITY
UNABLE
UPLIFTED
UMBRELLA
COOLER
UNDERPASS
URN
ULTIMATE
UNITED
UNBELIEVABLE
UNGUARDED
UNCLEAN
UNCIVIL
UNEQUAL
UPPER
UDDER
UNIVERSE
UNCURL
UNBIDDEN
UNICORN
UNIFY
UNDER
UNCORK
UPROOT
UPON
USUAL
UNCOVER
UNCUT
UTENSIL
UPWARD
UPSTAIRS
ULCER
UNBLOCK
UNTIE
UNLOVED
UNCONSCIOUS
UNCLE
UTOPIA
UKULELE
UNBEND
USED
URGE
UTTER
UNCOUTH
UNBUCKLE
UNDERWEAR
UNUSUAL
US
ULNA
URCHIN
UPTOWN
URBAN
USHER
UNCHAINED
URGENT
UNTIL
ULTERIOR
UNBOUND
UPROAR
UNITY
UPSET
UPPERCUT
UGUISU
USEFUL
GIG 2016

Ww

WAGON
WIMPLE
WHACK
WHARF
WHILE
WITCHY
WEED
WARMTH
WATTLE
WEIGHT
31 of 56

WHELP
WHIFF
WHIPPLE
WOMAN
WALLET
WARP
WHERE
WHY
WHEN
WRENCH
WATERFRONT

WARD
WASHER
WOW
WHO
WHAT
WEDGE
WRING
WRITE

WITCH
WELD
WILLOW
WINCE
WIZEN
WAX
WISDOM
WOODEN
WARRANT
WALL
WAR
WAVY
WINDMILL
WHITE
WHOOP
WEATHER
WANT
WANDER
WARLORD
WAY
WEB
WALRUS
WROTE
WORRY
WRATHFUL
WARTHOG
WEALTH
WINDOW
WATERPROOF
WATERHORSE
WINTER
WIND

WHITE TIGER
WHOPPER
WORLD
WHITTLE
WHIP
WANE
WHOLESOME
WISP
WIPERS
WAVE
WADED

WEB
WAPITI
WHISKER
WICKER
WEAVE
WRING
WHENCE
WRIST
WHOLE
WEIRD
WRATH
WITHER
WRECK
WIRE
WINGS
WESTWING
WHITE
WINE
WALLFLOWER

WARDROBE
WIG
WRY
WINDOW
WOLF
WOOL
WORST
WONDER
WINK
WHISTLE
WEEVIL
WILDERNESS
WATERMELON
MEEK
WOBBLE
WIPED
WASTED
WINDY
WAND
WISHINGWELL
WATER DRAGON

WEASEL
WELCOME
WORM
WIFE
WILL
WIDOW
WHIZ
WEARY
WASP
WEAN
WARPED
WEDNESDAY
WALKWAY
WIENER
WORLDWIDE
WHEELCHAIR
WOKEN
WROUGHT
WOLVERINE
WICK
WALLOP
WRONG

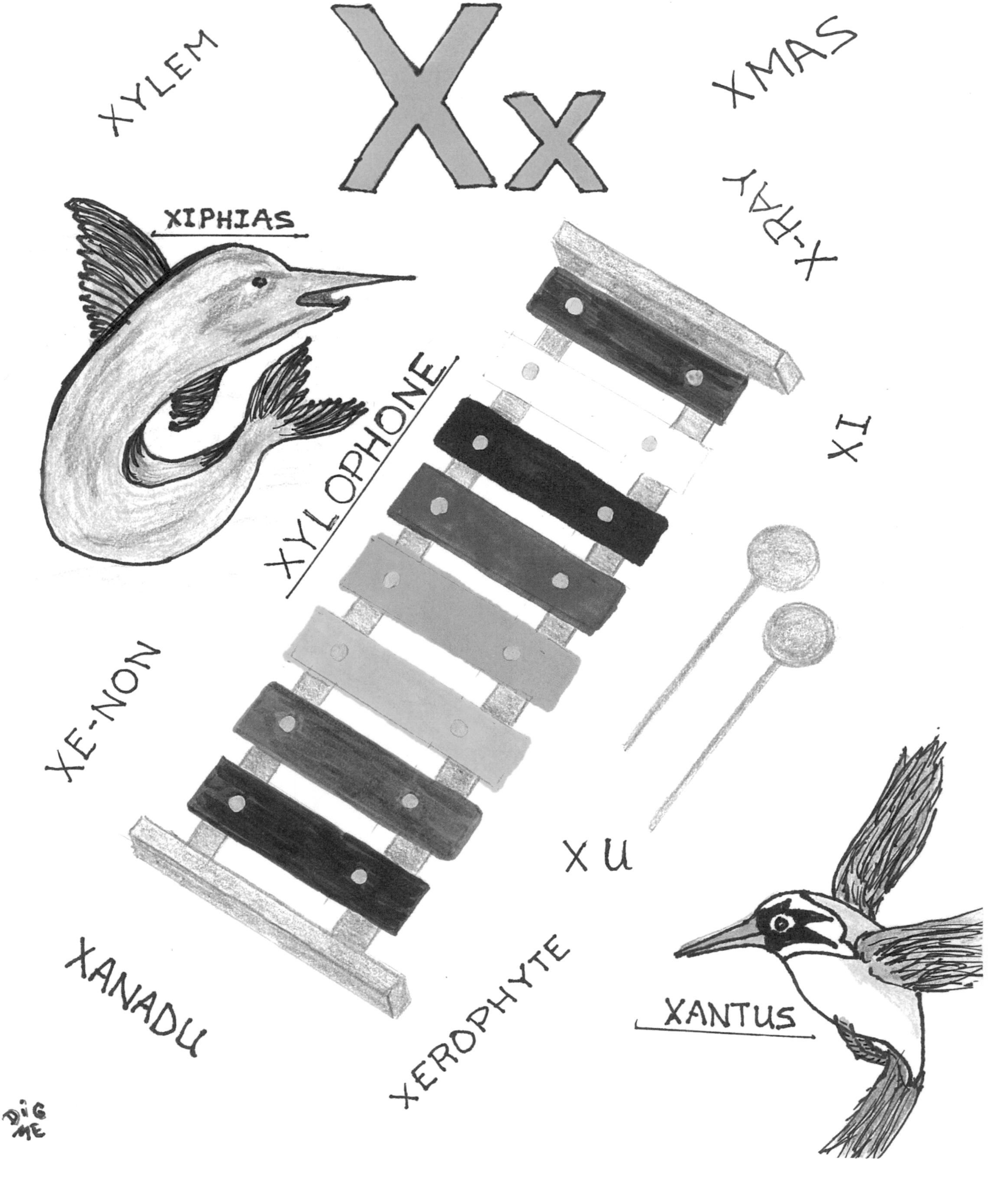

XYLEM

XMAS

X-RAY

Xx

XIPHIAS

XYLOPHONE

XI

XE-NON

XU

XANADU

XEROPHYTE

XANTUS

DIG
ME

Yy

YEAR
YOGA
YOKE
YOLK
YOUTHFUL

YELLOWEYE
PENGUIN

YETI

YUMMY
YUP
YACHT
YAW
YORE
YURT

YARDSTICK
1 foot | 2 foot | 3 foot

YUCCA
YOWL

YULE
YES
YOUTH
YOURSELF
YELP

YOWIE
YIKES
YODEL
YAWN
YET
YANKEE
YOGURT

YIELD
YEARN
YOUNG
YELLOW
FINCH

YEN
YAP
YOUR
YELL
YEAST

YUCKY
YEA
YOYO
YARD
YEARLING

YELLOW
YAMMER
YESTERDAY

YAK

DiME

Zz

ZIT
ZINE
ZONKED
ZINGER
ZIRCON
ZEE
ZEPHYR
ZED
ZEN
ZINGER
ZWIEBACK
HEINZ
ZEPPELIN
ZONAL
ZEAL
ZIT
ZIPPER
ZOOM
ZEBU
ZITI
ZOWIE
ZEAL
ZOO
ZINC
ZINE
ZOYSIA
ZAG
ZEBRA
ZOOT
ZEALOUS
ZESTY
ZUCCHINI
ZOMBIE
ZULU
ZAP
ZING
ZEST
ZIG
ZOW
ZERO
ZIP
ZONE
ZAPPED
ZITHER
ZINGER
ZODIAC
ZILLION
ZANY
ZOUNDS
ZOOLOGY

DiG
ME

A

Aardvark
About
Abyss
Ace
Acorn
Action
Add
Afire
After
Afterthought
Aggravate
Air
Alivia
All
All
Alligator
Allowance
Along
Also
Always
Am
Amaryllis
Amaze
Ambition
Amble
Amen
American
Amid
Amiss
Ammonia
Amnesia
Amoeba
Amok
Among
Among
Amulet

Amuse
Amy
Anatomy
Anchor
Anew
Angel
Anger
Anger
Angle
Angle
Animal
Annex
Another
Ant Anteater
Anterior Anthrax
Antman
Anxiety
Anxious
Any
Apathy
Ape
Aphid
Apology
Apostle
Appeal
Appear
Appendix
Apple
Apply
Apron
Are
Arm
Army
Article
Artificial
Ascot
Ascot

Ash
Ashes
Ask
Asp
Assault
Assay
Assemble
Asterisk
Asthma
Astrology
Aunt
Automobile
Avengers
Aviator
Avocado
Awful
Ax
Axle
Aye
Axle
Aye

B

Backwards
Bad
Bald
Ball
Ballroom
Bamboo
Banana
Band
Bandaid
Banjo
Bank
Barber
Barn
Basin

Basketball
Bass
Bassinet
Bat
Bay
Beard
Beautiful
Bed
Bee
Beg
Believe
Below
Bench
Big
Bird
Blood
Blue
Blueberry
Boa
Boat
Bomb
Boost
Boot
Border
Bottom
Bounce
Bound
Bow
Bowl
Bowling ball
Box
Boy
Branch
Brand
Bread
Brick
Bridge

Brief
Briefly
Bright
Brine
Bring
Brood
Bud
Buddy
Buffalo
Bug
Build
Bulk
Bullet
Bulletin
Bully
Bump
Bumper
Bundle
Burst
Business
Busy
But
Butcher
Butter
Butterfly
Buttons
Buy
Buzzer
By
Bye

C

Call
Can
Cancel
Candle
Cannot

Car
Cards
Cart
Castle
Cat
Caterpillar
Cellar
Cent
Chace
Chagrin
Chain
Chair
Chalice
Chalk
Challenge
Chamber
Champ
Champ
Chance
Change
Channel
Chapter
Char
Charcoal
Chart
Chase
Chasm
Chat
Checker
Cheek
Cheer
Cheese
Chef
Chemical
Cherish
Chicken
Child

Chili
Chill
Chime
Chimp
China
Chive
Chloroform
Choir
Choke
Choose
Chore
Christmas
Church
Cider
Cinch
Circumstance
Circus
Citrus
City
Civilize
Class
Climb
Club
Coal
Coffee
Cole
Collar
Collect
Color
Comb
Comet
Compare
Consume
Cow
Crackers
Credit
Crown

Cup
Cupboard
Cut
Cute

D

Dad
Daisy
Danger
Darn
Dave
Dawn
Day
Deadline
Deaf
Deal
Dean
Debate
Debt
Decent
Decide
Decimal
Decision
Deck
Declare
Decorate
Deed
Deer
Delight
Delivery
Delta
Demo
Deposit
Depth
Deputy
Derby
Design

Desire
Desk
Desolate
Desperate
Detonate
Devil
Diagram
Diamond
Dictate
Diet
Difficult
Dig
Dill
Dim
Dime
Dinner
Dinosaur
Dirt
Disco
Disease
Dish
Distance
Distant
Distress
Dive
Divide
Do
Doctor
Does
Dog
Dollar
Dom
Dome
Dominion
Domino
Don
Donation

Done
Donkey
Door
Dose
Dot
Double
Dove
Down
Doze
Drab
Draft
Drag
Dragon
Dragonfly
Drastic
Draw
Dream
Dress
Dresser
Drink
Drum
Drunk
Dryer
Dub
Duck
Duel
Dug
Duke
Dumb
Dynamite

E

Each
Eager
Eagle
Earl
Early

Earrings
Earth
East
Easter
Easy
Eat
Ebb
Ebony
Echo
Eclipse
Ecology
Eddy
Education
Eel
Eerie
Efficient
Effort
Eggs
Ego
Egret
Egyptian
Eighty
Either
Eject
Eke
Elastic
Elate
Elbow
Elder
Elect
Electric
Elementary
Elephant
Elevator
Eleven
Elf
Eliminate

Elixir
Elk
Elope
Elude
Emanate
Embrace
Emcee
Emergency
Emir
Emit
Emory
Emote
Emphasis
Empire
Employ
Empty
Emu
Enclose
Encourage
End
Endow
Enough
Enter
Entertain
Entry
Epic
Epidemic
Equator
Equine
Ermine
Erode
Erosion
Errand
Error
Erupt
Espy
Essay

Ethical
Evade
Eve
Ever
Everyone
Excel
Excite
Excuse
Exit
Express
Extra
Extract
Eye

F

Fairy
Falcon
Fall
False
Famous
Fancy
Fat
Father
Favorite
Fear
Feared
Feather
February
Feel
Feeler
Feet
Fellow
Ferret
Few
Fewer
Fib
Fig

Fight
Figure
Filler
Filly
Fin
Fine
Finger
Fire
Fish
Fit
Fix
Flag
Flake
Flamingo
Flash
Flew
Flight
Flip
Flop
Floss
Flounder
Flower
Flub
Food
Fool
Foot
Fop
Force
Forceful
Fork
Form
Forward
Fountain
Fox
Freaky
Freeze
Fritter

Frog
From
Front
Frontier
Frown
Fudge
Full
Fuller
Fumble
Fume
Fungus
Funny
Furry
Future
Fuzzy

G

Gag
Gale
Gallery
Gallop
Galoshes
Game
Gap
Gar
Garden
Gargle
Garland
Garment
Gas
Gate
Gecko
Gel
Gene
General
Genius
Gentle

Genuine
Geography
Geranium
Germ
Get
Geyser
Ghost
Gibbon
Gift
Gigantic
Giggle
Giraffe
Girl
Give
Given
Glad
Glance
Glass
Gleam
Globe
Glory
Glove
Gnome
Go
Gobbler
God
Golf
Good
Goop
Goose
Gopher
Gorge
Gorilla
Gospel
Got
Government
Grace

Graduate
Grapes
Grass
Grave
Gray
Great
Green
Grill
Grime
Growth
Grub
Guard
Guide
Guilty
Gum
Gumdrop
Gun
Guppy
Gush
Gymnasium
Gypsy

H

Habit
Hail
Hair
Half
Hallow
Halloween
Halo
Hamlet
Hammer
Hamper
Hand
Hank
Hash
Hatchet

Head
Headdress
Heave
Heaven
Heavy
Help
Herb
Hero
Hero
Hickory
Hieroglyphics
Highest
Hike
Hill
Him
Himalayas
Hind
Hinder
Hindu
Hip
Hippopotamus
History
Hit
Hoax
Hobble
Hockey
Hoe
Hog
Hoist
Hold
Hole
Holly
Holy
Homage
Home
Homework
Honest

Honey
Honor
Hood
Hook
Hoop
Hoot
Hopscotch
Horizon
Horrid
Horse
Horseradish
Hospital
Hot
Hotel
Hound
House
Hover
Hub
Hue
Hug
Hulk
Human
Humble
Humid
Hummingbird
Humorous
Hump
Hunk
Hunter
Hurrah
Hurricane
Hurry
Hush
Hut
Hutch
Hydrogen
Hyena

Hygiene
Hype

I

Ibis
Ice cream
Icicle
Iconic
Idea
Idiot
IF
Igloo
Ignite
Ignore
Iguana
Ilk
Ill
Image
Imagine
Immediate
Immigrant
Imp
Impair
Impala
Impel
Impending
Impolite
Imposing
Impossible
Impress
Imprint
In
Inch
Include
Indeed
Index
Indian

Inform
Infuse
Ink
Innocent
Inscribe
Insect
Insolent
Inspect
Inspire
Instant
Instead
Instruct
Integrity
Intend
Interest
Interfere
Internet
Interrupt
Into
Intrude
Invent
Investigation
Invite
Invoice
Invoke
Iris
Irish
Iron
Is
Island
Issue
It
Itch
Item
Ivy

J

Jab
Jabber
Jackal
Jacket
Jackknife
Jacks
Jade
Jaguar
Jail
Jake
Jalapeno
Jalopy
Jam
Jamb
January
Japan
Jape
Jar
Jasmine
Jaunt
Java
Jaw
Jay
Jazz
Jeans
Jeep
Jeepers
Jeezopete
Jello
Jelly
Jellybeen
Jellyfish
Jerk
Jerkin
Jerkingly
Jess

Jest
Jesus
Jet
Jewel
Jib
Jiggle
Jigsaw
Jilly
Jilt
Jimmy
Jingle
Jinx
Jitterbug
Job
Jock
Jockey
Joey
John
Johnnycake
Join
Joke
Joker
Jolly
Jolt
Jostled
Jot
Journal
Joy
Judge
Judy
Juice
Jukebox
July
Jumprope
June
Jungle
Junior

Junk
Jury
Just
Justice
Jut

K

Kabob
Kaboom
Kaiser
Kale
Kaleidoscope
Kamikaze
Kangaroo
Kaoline
Karaoke
Karat
Karate
Karma
Karst
Katydid
Kayak
Kazoo
Kedge
Keel
Keen
Keep
Keg
Kelly
Ken
Kennel
Keratin
Kerchief
Kernels
Kerosene
Kestrel
Ketch

Kettle

Key

Khaki

Kibble

Kibbutz

Kibosh

Kick

Kickboxer

Kid

Kidding

Kidney

Kidney Bean

Kidney pie

Kielbasa

Kill

Kiln

Kilo

Kilogram

Kilt

Kimino

Kin

Kind

Kindergarten

Kindle kindling

King

Kink

Kiosk

Kipper

Kirtle

Kismet

Kiss

Kit

Kitchen

Kite

Kith

Kitten

Kiwi

Klutz

Knell

Knife

Knight

Knob

Knock

Knocker

Knoll

Knot

Know

Knowledge

Knuckle

Koala

Kook

Kooky

Kosher

Koy

Kraut

Krypton

Kudos

Kudzu

Kumquat

Kungfu

L

Labrador

Ladybug

Lamp

Lamplight

Lay

Leaf

Leap

Lemer

Lemon

Leud

Lever

Liar

Liberal

Liberate

Library

Lied

Lift

Light

Like

Lilac

Lilt

Limabean

Limber

Lime

Limited

Linda

Linear

Lingo

Link

Lion

Lioness

Lionfish

Lips

Liquid

Liquidate

List

Lit

Literal

Liver

Livid

Living

Llama

Loaf

Loan

Lobby

Lobster

Localized

Lock

Locket

Locomotion

Lode

Lodge

Lofty

Logically

Loiter

Lollipop

Lonely

Long

Longitude

Loofah

Look

loopy

loosen

lord

Lose

loss

lot

lothe

lottery

lotus

loud

lounge

Lousy

lout

love

lovely

low

Lowest

lox

Lozenge

lucid

lucky

luggage

lull

Lullaby

lumber

luminous
lump
Lunatic
lunch
Lung
Lurch

M

Macaroni
Macaw
Machete
Machine
Mad
Madam
Made
Madonna
Maestro
Magazine
Magenta
Maggot
Magician
Magistrate
Magnesium
Magnetic
Magnify
Mail
Maim
Major
Malamute
Maleficent
Mallet
Maltese
Manacle
Manatee
Maneuver
Manicure
Mantaray

Mars
Marshal
Mary
Material
Matt
Mature
May
Mayor
Me
Measure
Medicine
Melancholy
Meld
Mellow
Melon
Melt
Membrane
Memorable
Memory
Mentality
Mention
Menu
Mercury
Mercy
Mere
Merry
Message
Meter
Metric
Microwave
Middle
Midge
Mighty
Milk
Millionaire
Mind
Minded

Mine
Minute
Minx
Miracle
Mirage
Mirror
Mischief
Misery
Mission
Mistake
Mix
Mizzen
Mob
Model
Mohawk
Moisture
Molasses
Molecule
Monday
Money
Monk
Monkey
Monocle
Monster
Month
Mood
Morning
Morph
Mortality
Mortgage
Mote
Mother
Motto
Mouse
Movie
Muggy
Mumps

Muscle
Muse
Mushroom
Mutant
Muzzle
Myself
Mystery

N

Nacho
Nag
Naked
Name
Namely
Nanny
Nap
Narrow
Nasal
Nationalist
Native
Natty
Nature
Naughty
Nauseous
Naval
Navy
Near
Neatness
Necessary
Neck
Necklace
Nectar
Need
Needful
Needle
Negative
Neglect

Neigh
Neighbor
Neighborhood
Neither
Nemesis
Nephew
Nerd
Nerve
Nervous
Nestle
Net
Neutralize
Neutron
Newfoundlander
Newspaper
Newt
Next
Nexus
Nib
Niche
Nickle
Niece
Nifty
Night
Nightingale
Nightmare
Nikki
Nil
Nine
Ninja
Nip
Nit
Nitrogen
Nix
No
No one
Noble

Nobody
Noel
Noisy
Nonchalant
None
Nonsense
Noodle
Nook
Noon
Normal
North
Nostril
Nosy
Notch
Note
Nothing
Noun
Nova
Novel
November
Now
Noxious
Nozzle
Nubbin
Numb
Numbat
Number
Nurse
Nurture
Nut
Nutmeg
Nutrition
Nuzzle

O

Oaf
Oak

Oar
Oasis
Oat
Oath
Obedient
Obey
Obligation
Oblige
Oblivion
Obnoxious
Oboe
Obstacle
Occasion
Occure
Ocean
Ocelot
Octagon
October
Odd
Odyssey
Off
Offend
Office
Officer
Often
Ogle
Oh
Oil
Oink
Okay
Old
Oleo
Olives
Omega
Omen
Omission
Omnibus

Omnivorous
Once
One
Onion
Only
Onto
Onyx
Ooze
Opal
Opaque
Open
Opener
Opening
Opera
Operate
Operation
Opossum
Opponent
Oppress
Opt
Optimism
Opulent
Oracle
Oral
Orange
Orangutan
Orate
Orchestra
Orchid
Ordeal
Order
Ordinary
Ore
Oregano
Organic
Organize
Osmosis

Osprey
Ostrich
Other
Otter
Ought
Ounce
Oust
Outburst
Outlaw
Outrage
Outside
Oval
Ovation
Owl
Ox
Oxide
Oxygen
Ozone

P

Pace
Package
Paddle
Paddock
Padlock
Page
Paint
Pair
Palate
Pale
Palm
Pan
Panda
Pansy
Panther
Paper
Par

Parachute
Parade
Paradox
Parallel
Parasite
Parasol
Parcel
Parlor
Parmesan
Parquet
Parrot
Particular
Partridge
Passage
Pasta
Pastor
Pastrami
Pastry
Pat
Patched
Patomine
Pattern
Patty
Paw
Peach
Peanut
Pear
Peel
Peg
Pelican
Pen
Penguin
Penny
Pent
Pepper
Pepperoni
Pickup

Pie
Pig
Pigeon
Pile
Pilgrim
Pill
Pillar
Pineapple
Pipe
Pirate
Pizza
Plum
Pod
Point
Pointer
Pole
Poster
Pox
Prairie
Pray
Pretty
Prize
Promise
Public
Pueblo
Puffy
Pully
Pumpkin
Punch
Purple
Push
Put

Q

Qat
Qatar
Qed

Qinnant
Qiviut
Quack
Quad
Quadrangle
Quadrant
Quadruple
Quaff
Quail
Quaint
Quake
Qualified
Quality
Qualm
Quamash
Quandary
Quark
Quarrel
Quarry
Quart
Quarter
Quarterback
Quartet
Quartz
Quasar
Quashed
Quaver
Quay
Queasy
Queen
Queer
Quell
Query
Question mark
Quetzal
Queue
Quey

Quiche
Quick
Quid
Quiet
Quilt
Quince
Quinine
Quintal
Quintar
Quintuplet
Quire
Quirk
Quit
Quite
Quiver
Quiz
Quoit
Quota
Quotation
Quote
Quotient

R

Rabbi
Rabbit
Raccoon
Rack
Radar
Radiate
Radio
Radiology
Radish
Radius
Raffle
Rag
Rage
Raid

Rail
Railroad
Rainbow
Raise
Rake
Rampant
Rap
Rappel
Raptor
Rare
Rascal
Rational
Rattan
Rattlesnake
Raucous
Rave
Raven
Ravish
Raw
Raze
Razor
Reach
React
Read
Ready
Rebel
Receipt
Receive
Recess
Recite
Recognize
Recommend
Recount
Recover
Recruit
Rectangle
Recuperate

Recycle
Red
Redeem
Reef
Reel
Reflect
Reflex
Reform
Regal
Regular
Reject
Relapse
Relative
Reliable
Relic
Rely
Remote
Renovate
Rental
Repair
Repast
Repay
Repent
Report
Represent
Reptile
Reputation
Repute
Rescue
Research
Resign
Rhinoceros
Road
Rogue
Roman
Romp
Roof

Rooster
Root
Rosary
Rose
Rotate
Rough
Rove
Row
Rubberband
Ruby
Rug
Rum
Runt

S

Sack
Sad
Saddle
Sag
Sago
Said
Saintly
Salamander
Salt
Salve
Salvo
Sanctify
Sandpaper
Sapphire
Satyr
Saucer
Sausage
Savannah
Savor
Savory
Sawdust
Saxophone

Scab
Scales
Scarce
Scared
Scatter
Scavenger
Scheme
Schism
Scholar
School
Science
Scoff
Scold
Scoop
Scooter
Scorn
Scout
Scrape
Scratch
Screech
Screw
Script
Scud
Seahorse
Seashell
Season
Seat
Seaweed
Second
Section
Secure
Sedan
Seed
Seesaw
Segregate
Selfish
Sell

Semi
Seminar
Senior
Separate
Server
Seven
Seventy
Sew
Shaker
Shameless
Sharp
Shave
She
Shed
Sheep
Shelf
Sheriff
Shrub
Sift
Sign
Sill
Silly
Silo
Silver
Sip
Sit
Six
Skeleton
Ski
Skirt
Slang
Slope
Smile
Snowy owl
Soap
Social
Sofa

Soft
Sop
Sphynx
Spider
Spring
Square
Squirrel
Statue
Steak
String
Sue
Sufficient
Sugar
Sunday
Sunshine

T

Table Tennis
Taboo
Tackle
Tailor
Talisman
Tallow
Tam
Tang
Tapioca
Tardy
Tarnish
Tarpon
Tasmanian devil
Tattoo
Tavern
Tax
Teach
Teapot
Technical
Teddy bear

Telegram
Telephone
Telescope
Tell
Temper
Temperature
Temple
Tempo
Tendon
Tent
Terminal Terrace
Territory
Testify
Tetra
Thanksgiving
Them
Therapy
Thermos
These
They
Thought
Thousand
Throne
Thrown
Thumb
Thunder
Thursday
Tiara
Ticket
Tiger
Tile
Timber
Tip
Tire
Titanic
Title
Tizzy

To	Trench	Uguisu	Unicycle
Toad	Trend	Ukulele	Unify
Toast	Triangle	Ulcer	Unique
Tobogan	Trick	Ulna	United
Toddler	Tricycle	Ulterior	Unity
Toe	Trilogy	Ultimate	Universe
Toga	Triton	Ultra	Unloved
Together	Trivial	Umbrella	Unpredictable
Toilet	Trouble	Umrellabird	Untangle
Token	Trout	Unable	Untie
Tolerate	Truck	Unanimous	Until
Tom	Trump	Unbelievable	Unzip
Tom Tom	Truth	Unbend	Uplifted
Tomato	Tube	Unbidden	Upon
Tongue	Tuesday	Unblock	Upper
Tonsils	Tug	Unbound	Uppercut
Too	Tulips	Unbuckle	Uproar
Topiary	Tumble	Uncanny	Uproor
Torch	Tune	Unchained	Upset
Tortoise	Tunic	Uncivil	Upstairs
Torture	Turmoil	Uncle	Uptown
Tot	Turret	Unclean	Upward
Tote	Tutor	Uncommon	Uranium
Toucan	Tweed	Unconscious	Urban
Tournament	Tweet	Uncouth	Urchin
Tow	Tweezers	Uncover	Urge
Toward	Twelve	Uncurl	Urgent
Toxic	Twilight	Uncut	Urology
Tractor	Twin	Under	Ursa
Traffic	Twine	Underfoot	Us
Transform	Twinkle	Underground	Use
Trash	Two	Understand	Used
Travel	Type	Underwear	Useful
Treasure		Unequal	Usher
Treat	**U**	Unguarded	Utensil
Tree		Unhappy	Utility
Tremble	Udder	Unicorn	Utilized
	Ugly		

Utopia
Utter

V

Vacant
Vacate
Vacation
Vacuum
Vagabond
Vagrant
Vague
Vain
Vale
Valentine
Valise
Valor
Valuable
Value
Valve
Vamp
Vampire
Van
Vandal
Vane
Vanilla
Vanity
Vantage
Vapor
Varied
Varmint
Varnish
Vary
Vase
Vassal
Vault
Veal
Vegan

Vegetable
Vehicle
Veil
Vein
Veld
Velvet
Vend
Veneer
Venison
Venom
Vent
Venture
Veranda
Verbal
Verge
Verify
Vermin
Verse
Version
Vertebra
Vertigo
Verve
Very
Vessel
Vest
Vet
Veteran
Veto
Vex
Vibe
Vibrate
Vise
Vicinity
Victim
Victor
Video
Vie

View
Vigil
Vigor
Viking
Vile
Vine
Vinegar
Vinyl
Viola
Violence
Violin
Viral
Virgin
Virtue
Virus
Visa
Visage
Vision
Visual
Vital
Vitamin
Viva
Vixen
Vizier
Vocabulary
Vocal
Voice
Void
Volcano
Vomit
Vortex
Vote
Vow
Voyage
Vulgar
Vulture

W

Waded
Wagon
Walkway
Wallet
Wallop
Walrus
Wand
Wane
Want
War
Warble
Ward
Wardrobe
Warlord
Warmth
Warp
Warped
Warrant
Warthog
Washer
Wasp
Wasted
Waterfront
Watermelon
Waterproof
Wattle
Wavy
Way
Wax
Way
Wealth
Wean
Weary
Weasel
Weather
Weave

Web
Wedge
Wednesday
Weed
Week
Weevil
Weight
Weird
Welcome
Weld
Westwing
Whack
Wharf
What
Wheelchair
Whelp
When
Whence
Where
Which
Whiff
While
Whip
Whisker
Whistle
White
White tiger
Whittle
Whiz
Who
Whole
Wholesome
Whoop
Whopper
Why
Wick
Widow

Wiener
Wife
Wig
Wilderness
Will
Willow
Wimple
Wince
Wind
Windmill
Window
Wine
Wink
Winter
Wiped
Wipers
Wire
Wisdom
Wicked
Witch
Wither
Wizen
Wolf
Wolverine
Woman
Wonder
Wooden
Wool
Worldwide
Worm
Worry
Worse
Worst
Worth
Wow
Wrap
Wrath

Wreck
Wrench
Wring
Wrist
Write
Wrong
Wrote
Wrought
Wrung
Wry

X

Xanadu
Xantus
Xenon
Xerophyte
Xi
Xiphias
Xmas
Xray
Xu
Xylophone

Y

Yelp
Yen
Yes
Yesterday
Yet
Yeti
Yikes
Yoga
Yogurt
Yoke
Yolk
Yore

Young
Your
Yourself
Youth
Yowie
Yowl
Yoyo
Yucca
Yucky
Yule
Yup
Yurt

Z

Zag
Zap
Zeal
Zealous
Zebra
Zebu
Zed
Zee
Zen
Zenith
Zephyr
Zeppelin
Zero
Zest
Zesty
Zig
Zillion
Zin
Zinc
Zine
Zinger
Zip
Zipper

Zircon
Zit
Zither
Ziti
Zodiac
Zombie
Zone
Zonked
Zoo
Zoology
Zoom
Zoot
Zounds
Zow
Zowie
Zoysia
Zucchini
Zwieback

About the Author

Mary Woodman born and raised in Michigan now lives in Florida. Has born three children. Has 10 grandchildren, 3 great grandchildren. Loves reading, writing and drawing. She is now 71 years old, with the goal to write more books.

Printed in the United States
by Baker & Taylor Publisher Services